Napkin Folding

by Irena Chalmers

drawings by B. Penny

published by

Potpourri Press

P. O. BOX 10312
GREENSBORO, N. C. 27404

Table Of Contents

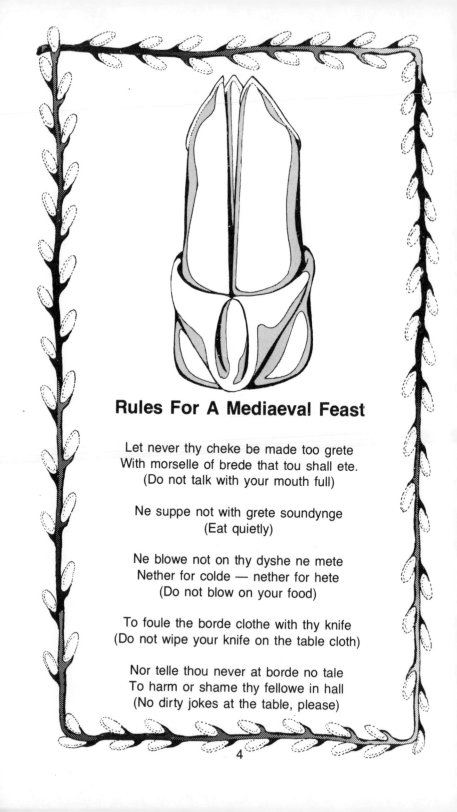

Rules For A Mediaeval Feast

Let never thy cheke be made too grete
With morselle of brede that tou shall ete.
(Do not talk with your mouth full)

Ne suppe not with grete soundynge
(Eat quietly)

Ne blowe not on thy dyshe ne mete
Nether for colde — nether for hete
(Do not blow on your food)

To foule the borde clothe with thy knife
(Do not wipe your knife on the table cloth)

Nor telle thou never at borde no tale
To harm or shame thy fellowe in hall
(No dirty jokes at the table, please)

Introduction

Table decorating is the fine art of creating a tasteful setting for the guests, the food and the wine, so that each is accorded its own importance. Imagination is of far greater value than unlimited funds whether the occasion is formal, with hothouse flowers, sparkling crystal, fragile bone china and double damask dinner napkins, or a gathering for family and close friends, when the table is set with earthenware and paper napkins. Two chrysanthemums and a gracefully curved branch can be more breathtakingly beautiful than a florist's interpretation of an "arrangement."

The accessories for decorating the table often suggest themselves; at the beach, a few summer roses tucked into back to back spiral-shaped sea shells make a splendid centerpiece and grey-silver abalone or scallop shells may be used for serving the hors' d'oeuvres. The napkins, blue, green or coral colored are folded simply and the food will be fresh and uncomplicated.

A candlelight supper for two could be served on a crisp black linen tablecloth with pewter and smoked grey glasses, plates and goblets. Three or four anemones or daffodils with a few windswept twigs of forsythia or pussywillow create their own ambiance for elegant foods and splendid wine.

Gold lacquered individual serving trays, bamboo place mats, rice bowls, chopsticks and fanned red napkins will enhance even take-out, brought-home Chinese food.

Improvisation and restraint go hand-in-hand when planning a table setting, and though beauty does not preclude comfort, being overly "clever" can spoil an effect completely.

One of the simplest ways of making an occasion out of a meal is to fold the napkins in ingenious ways. Many of the methods of folding are very simple, though, admittedly, others require a little dexterity until you get the knack of the thing.

The Napkins

It is easiest to work with new napkins; buy one to use for practicing.

Napkins must be starched if they are to be folded in fans or similar shapes in which they must support their own weight.

If the napkins are folded to lie flat on the table, they need not be starched.

It is simpler to work with square rather than rectangular shaped napkins.

Large folded napkins have a more dramatic impact than oft-laundered small napkins.

Patterned napkins may not be suitable for all the suggested designs, but before you give up, try folding them two or three times, you may be able to turn the fabric so that only the patterned side is showing.

It is considerably easier to fold napkins than it may first appear from looking at the illustrations.

Care Of Napkins

Wash all napkins separately in a cold water detergent.

If the napkin is stained with food or lipstick, stretch it tightly over a glass or small bowl and run cold water through the spot. Run very hot water through grease stains. If the mark is not removed, pour a few drops of liquid cold water detergent on the spot and rub it very gently. If it still refuses to budge, iron the fabric on top of a kitchen towel.

To remove red wine stains, soak the napkin in milk before attempting any other remedy. If you have already tried detergent, the milk idea will not work.

Iron napkins while they are still damp, or spray them with water from a plant atomizer. Use spray starch to give the fabric a satin smooth finish.

THE FORMAL DINNER

Although truly formal meals seem to be vanishing from to-day's scene, pushed from our lives by changing life styles and the lack of time, money and/or servants, there are still many times which such an event is demanded, either by the importance of the occasion or the guest(s) of honor... or desired, purely for the pleasure of dining elegantly and leisurely with good company, good food and wine and good service.

At home, you may choose to prepare in advance a completely formal setting, such as the one shown, so that when your guests enter the dining room, your table will appear at its lovliest, glistening with crystal and silver — a sight designed to delight the eye just as your menu is designed to please the palate. At other times, you may choose, as is more generally done, to use a basic setting for the first three courses, bringing additional utensils to the table with the appropriate courses.

Often, when dining out, you will find a complete setting when you arrive, the table having been pre-set to take care of all menu contingencies. After you have placed your order, however, the waiter will remove all unnecessary utensils.

For any formal dinner, the tablecloth should overhang the table by no less than sixteen inches and no more than twenty inches. If there is a crease down the center, the cloth should be spread crease side uppermost. Each setting is put one inch from the edge of the table and, for comfort, each setting should be at least 24 inches from the other.

Certain time-honored rules, which have evolved from the way food is served and eaten, govern the placement of flatware in what is really a most logical manner. It is placed one inch from the table edge in the order in which it will be used, knives (cutting edge facing toward the plate) and spoons to the right, and forks to the left. An exception to this is the small cocktail fork which, if used, is placed on the right outside the knives and spoons. Dessert utensils are placed horizontally at the top of the plate, such placement usually indicating that finger bowls will not be used. The butter spreader is placed horizontally across the butter plate as a rule, though in an extremely formal setting, it may be placed on the outside of the entrée forks.

A place plate, on the table when the guests are seated, may hold the napkin, beautifully folded in a design such as those included in this book, to further delight the eye. This plate is removed before the appetizer is served. If dinner opens with soup, the bowl may be put directly on the service plate, with both being removed before the fish course, which usually has been pre-arranged on separate plates, is served. Fish knives and forks, sometimes considered a pleasant anachronism, are still used in very formal settings and are placed, as you can see, in the correct course sequence. Originally made from bone, they absorbed the flavor of fish and it was customary to keep them separate from the all-purpose flatware.

When a poultry course is served, it follows next. Then, if desired, a Sorbet (or sherbet) course may precede the meat. The sorbet is not a sweet sherbet such as one bought in an ice cream store, but rather one made perhaps with some wine, or occasionally containing vegetable or fruit.

If the meat course is to be served directly to each guest, a plate, preferably heated, is placed before each person in preparation for service. If the meat is to be carved at the table, the platter is put in front of the host who places each serving as it is carved onto a hot plate which the server then places before each guest.

A salad or vegetable course comes next, which not only adds its own special flavor to the meal, but serves to clear the palate for more complete enjoyment of dessert and cheese. Often today, especially in the United States, the salad is served as a second course (in which case, the fork should be moved accordingly in the setting). However, in many restaurants and homes, both in the United States and Europe, where pure enjoyment of food remains of prime importance, the salad still follows the meat course. This is an alternative you may choose to try, and find a pleasant change, even though you are accustomed to serving salad earlier in the meal. If a salad with a vinegar dressing is used, wine should not be served, as the vinegar will distort the taste of the wine. A fruit compote, or similar dish, may be served in lieu of a salad, in which case a spoon is placed to the right in the setting and the salad fork on the left is eliminated.

If coffee is served, the demitasse spoon may be placed horizontally above the dessert and cheese utensils as shown, or may be put on the saucer behind the cup when it is placed to the right of each guest ready for the coffee to be served.

Water glasses often are not used when guests are serious wine drinkers, as wine and water are not compatible. If a water glass is used, it is placed slightly above the tip of the knife nearest the plate and in front of the wine glasses. It should be filled approximately two thirds full before guests are seated, while wine is poured at appropriate times during the meal.

If two wines are served, the white wine glass is placed closer to hand than the (usually larger) red wine glass. Although there are traditionally differently shaped glasses for different wines, many people now prefer to select a single all purpose wine glass, the best of which are large, to allow the wine to breathe, with a slightly rounded bowl to direct the fragrance of the wine to the nose of the recipient, and have a stem that is in balance with the dimension of the "cup." The glass must feel comfortable in your hand. Too large a glass is easily overturned and too small a glass is a sin against nature. All wine glasses should be absolutely clear so the color of the wine can be appreciated. The glass can be filled to slightly less than three fourths, but preferably to about half, of its capacity.

Liqueur, or a cordial, may be poured in the smaller glass shown after coffee is served, or if you choose, it may be passed on a tray later.

It is well to keep in mind the amount of help available to you when planning your menu. Without adequate people to serve, a strictly formal meal is impractical to attempt. A pleasant compromise may be effected with the use of a serving cart, on which advance courses may be placed ready for serving and on which plates from completed courses may be put. You may also choose to take advantage of the many aids — such as candle warmers, hot trays and insulated dishes or dishes with ice-billed bases — to help insure that hot food will reach the table hot and cold food will be served properly chilled.

As delightful as a formal dinner is, an informal one may be just as pleasing — and indeed, in today's society, may be preferable in many cases. In any event, it is a wise hostess who, knowing the facilities and help at her command, decides in advance the type of menu and service that will be most pleasant for everyone, never losing sight of the fact that the true spirit of hospitality is served only when the guests truly enjoy themselves. If this is the end result of any event you plan — whether it be a picnic in the park or a black tie dinner by candlelight, then you may relax in the sure knowledge that you have been a success!

Bishop's Hat

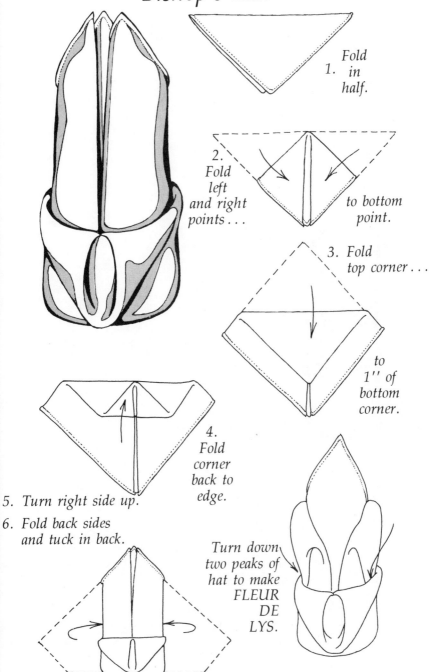

1. Fold in half.

2. Fold left and right points . . . to bottom point.

3. Fold top corner . . . to 1″ of bottom corner.

4. Fold corner back to edge.

5. Turn right side up.

6. Fold back sides and tuck in back.

Turn down two peaks of hat to make FLEUR DE LYS.

11

The Candle

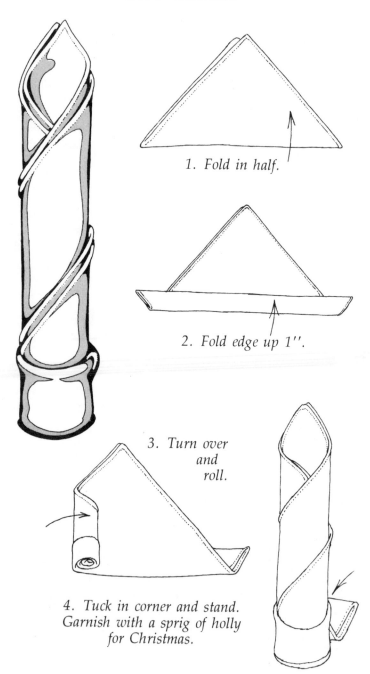

1. Fold in half.

2. Fold edge up 1″.

3. Turn over
and
roll.

4. Tuck in corner and stand.
Garnish with a sprig of holly
for Christmas.

Chelmsford

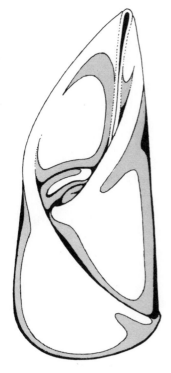

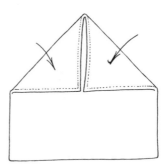

1. Fold top corners to center.

2. Fold bottom half up.

3. and down one half.

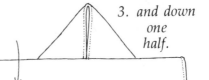

4. Fold sides to middle.

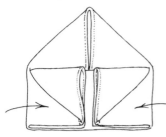

5. Fold in half and tuck in flap.

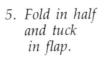

13

Cone

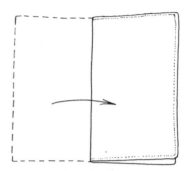

1. Fold in half.

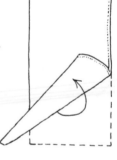

2. Roll into cone.

3. Fold bottom point up.

4. and fold up once again to make cuff.

14

Crown

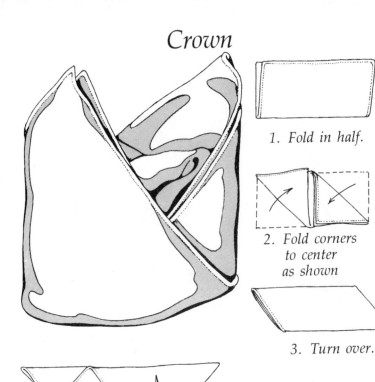

1. Fold in half.

2. Fold corners
   to center
   as shown

3. Turn over.

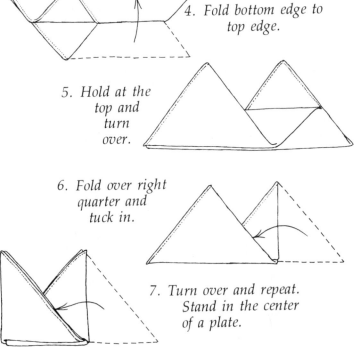

4. Fold bottom edge to
   top edge.

5. Hold at the
   top and
   turn
   over.

6. Fold over right
   quarter and
   tuck in.

7. Turn over and repeat.
   Stand in the center
   of a plate.

15

Lobster

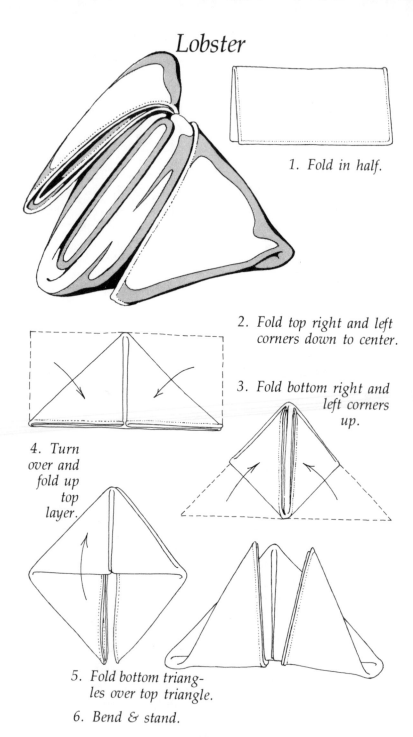

1. Fold in half.

2. Fold top right and left corners down to center.

3. Fold bottom right and left corners up.

4. Turn over and fold up top layer.

5. Fold bottom triangles over top triangle.

6. Bend & stand.

Muldevan

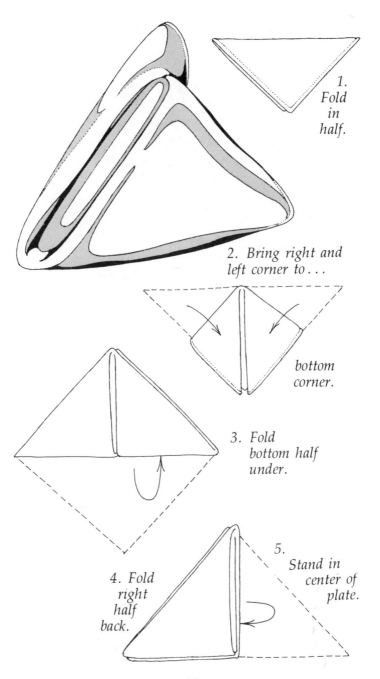

1. Fold in half.

2. Bring right and left corner to...

bottom corner.

3. Fold bottom half under.

4. Fold right half back.

5. Stand in center of plate.

17

Pinwheel

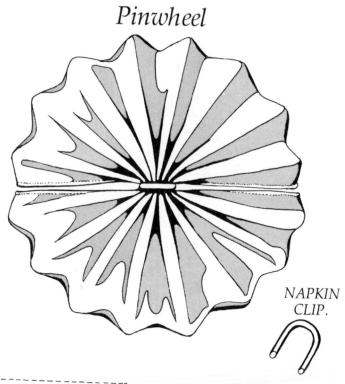

NAPKIN CLIP.

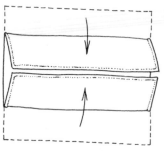

1. Fold top and bottom edge to center.

2. Fold from left to right in 1'' accordian pleats.

3. Clip in center.

4. Spread pinwheel.

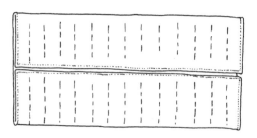

Pyramid

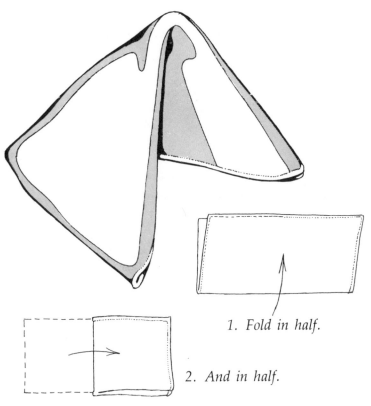

1. Fold in half.

2. And in half.

3. And in half again.

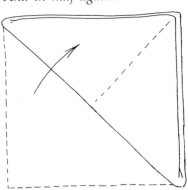

4. Bend
5. And
   stand
   upright,
   as shown
   at top.

Sailboat

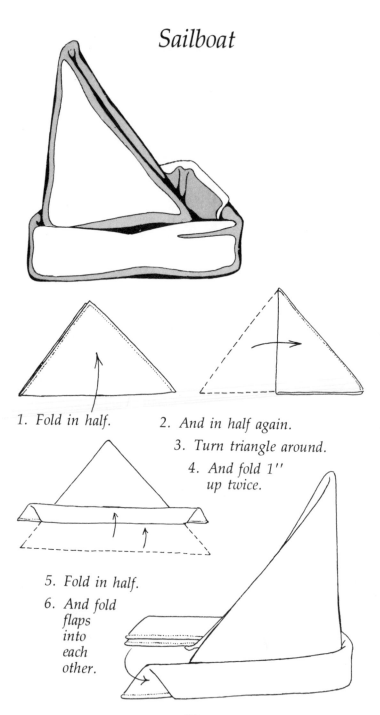

1. Fold in half.

2. And in half again.

3. Turn triangle around.

4. And fold 1″ up twice.

5. Fold in half.

6. And fold flaps into each other.

Standing Fan

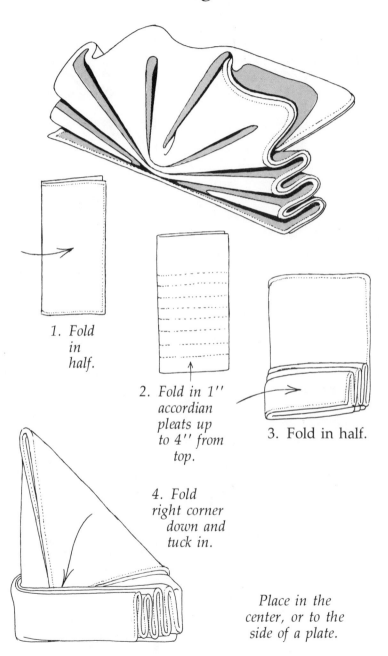

1. Fold in half.

2. Fold in 1'' accordian pleats up to 4'' from top.

3. Fold in half.

4. Fold right corner down and tuck in.

Place in the center, or to the side of a plate.

Ascot Tie

1. Fold in half.

2. Fold up one quarter.

3. And again one quarter.

4. Fold sides over.

5. Turn over.

Bonaparte

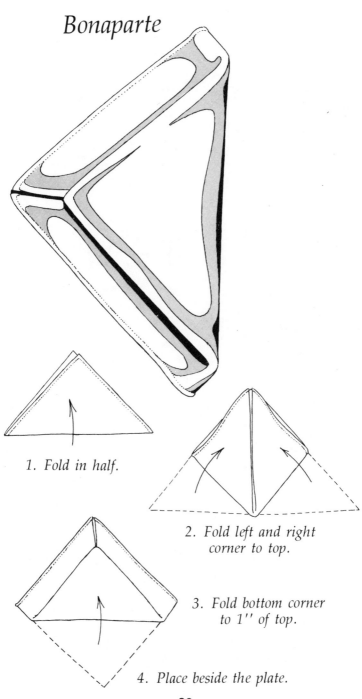

1. Fold in half.

2. Fold left and right corner to top.

3. Fold bottom corner to 1″ of top.

4. Place beside the plate.

The Book

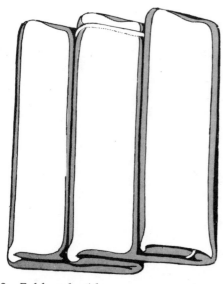

1. Fold in thirds.

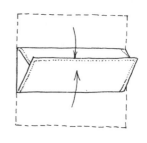

2. Fold each side over one quarter. 3. And bring ends to center.

4. Fold right side under.

5. And slide to make three even folds.

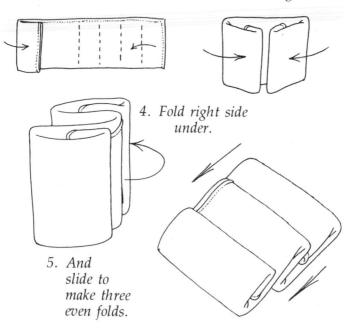

24

Buffet Server

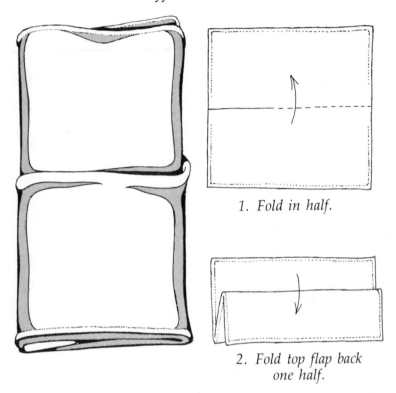

1. Fold in half.

2. Fold top flap back
   one half.

3. Turn over and fold into quarters.

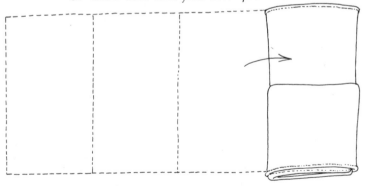

4. Insert utensils.

La Courte

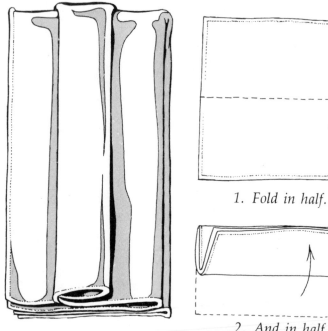

1. Fold in half.

2. And in half.

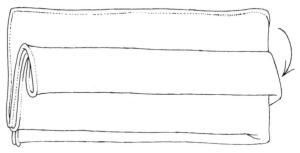

3. And in half again.

4. Fold top flap back one third.

Diagonal Stripe

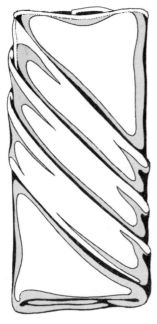

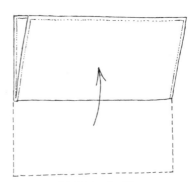

1. Fold in half.

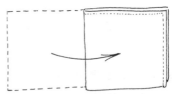

2. And in half again.

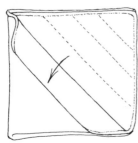

3. Fold
   down
   top flap.

4. Tuck in
   second
   and third
   flaps
   making
three even stripes.

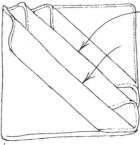

5. Turn
   back
   sides.

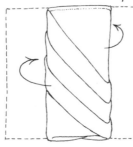

6. Insert
   card
   or
   flower.

27

Double Diamonds

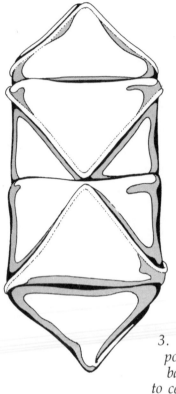

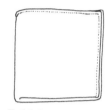

1. Fold into quarters.

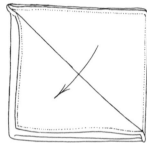

2. Fold back first flap.

3. Fold point back to center.

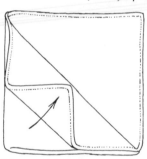

4. Fold second flap to center.

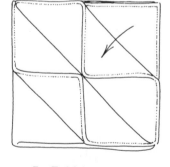

5. Fold back sides.

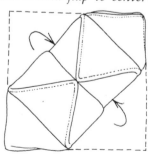

Empire

1. Fold into quarters.

2. Fold top flap down
   in quarters.

3. Fold second and third
flap. Tuck them in to make
                    three even
                       bands.

4. Fold back sides
and insert a flower or a card.

Geometric

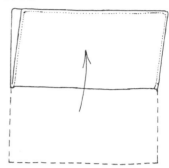

1. Fold in half.

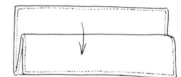

2. Fold top flap back
   one half.

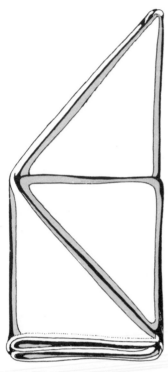

3. Turn over.

4. And bring left and
   right corners to center.

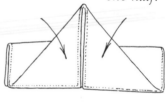

5. Fold over
   corner flaps.

6. Fold from
   right to left
   in quarters.

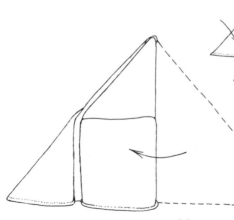

30

Gourmet

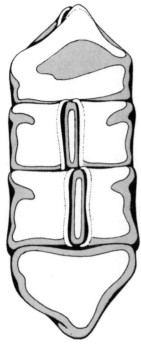

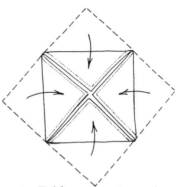

1. Fold corners to center.

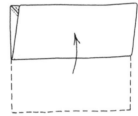

2. Fold in half.

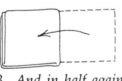

3. And in half again.

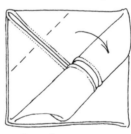

4. Fold first flap down.

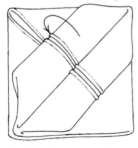

5. Tuck second flap under.

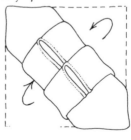

6. Fold back
    sides.

31

The Havanna

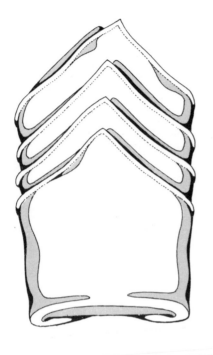

1. Fold into quarters.

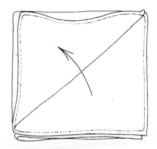

2. Fold first flap
   up one half.

3. Fold second flap up
   to 1'' of first. Repeat
   with third and fourth.

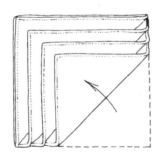

4. Fold back
   sides.

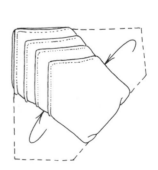

À La Maison

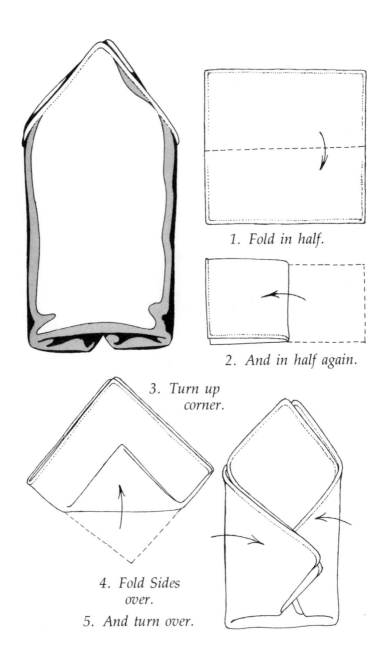

1. Fold in half.

2. And in half again.

3. Turn up corner.

4. Fold Sides over.

5. And turn over.

Special Buffet Server

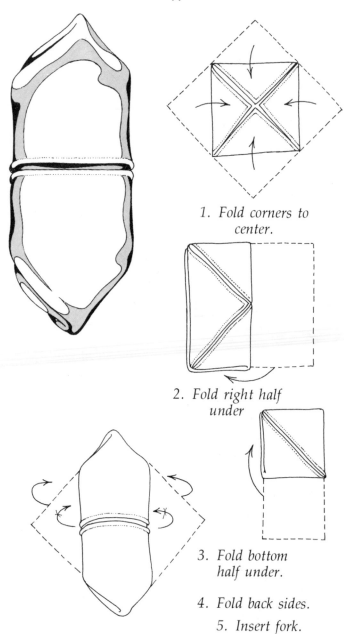

1. Fold corners to center.

2. Fold right half under

3. Fold bottom half under.

4. Fold back sides.

5. Insert fork.

Americana

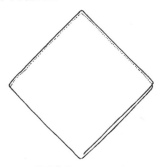

1. Fold into quarters.

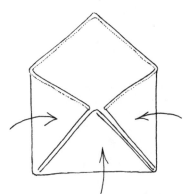

2. Fold bottom and sides to center.

3. Fold in thirds.

4. Slip on napking ring.

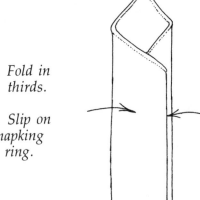

Bowtie

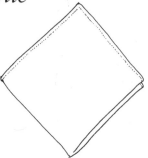

1. Fold in quarters.

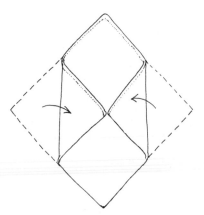

2. Fold sides to center.

3. Pleat in quarters.

4. Tie with ribbon
   or slip on ring.

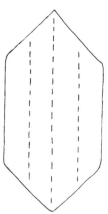

Scarf

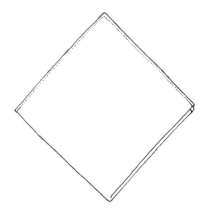

1. Fold into quarters.

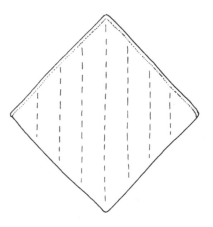

2. Fold in half and . . .

3. Pleat each half.

4. Slip on napkin ring.

Wand

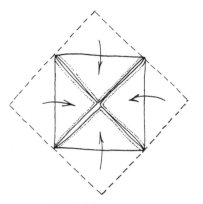

1. Fold corners
to center.

2. Fold
in
half.

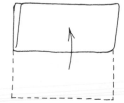

3. And in half again.

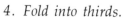

4. Fold into thirds.

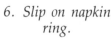

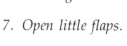

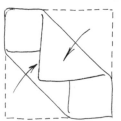

5. Fold in half.

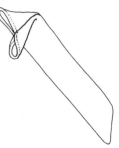

6. Slip on napkin
ring.

7. Open little flaps.

Fan

2. Pleat into one inch accordian pleats.

3. Slip into wine glass and spread fan.

1. Fold in half.

39

Lily

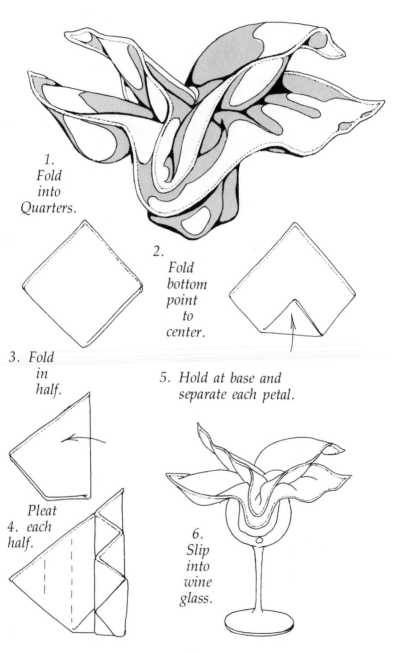

1.
Fold
into
Quarters.

2.
Fold
bottom
point
to
center.

3. Fold
in
half.

5. Hold at base and
separate each petal.

Pleat
4. each
half.

6.
Slip
into
wine
glass.

Rose

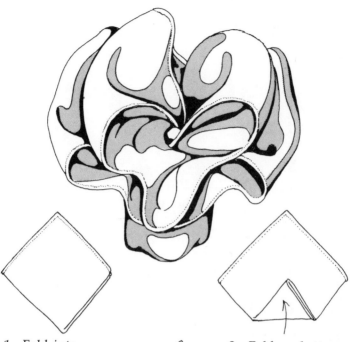

1. Fold into quarters.

2. Fold up bottom corner to center.

3. Fold in half.

4. Pleat each half.

5. Slip into wine glass.

6. Separate petals.

7. Tuck in each petal's point.

Swirl

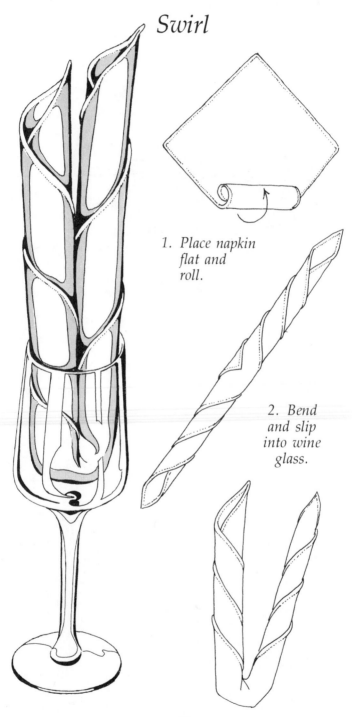

1. Place napkin
   flat and
   roll.

2. Bend
   and slip
   into wine
   glass.

Bottle Scarf

1. Fold in half.

2. Fold bottom edge up one quarter. And again one quarter.

3. Tie around the bottle.

4. Fold points to base.

Gondola

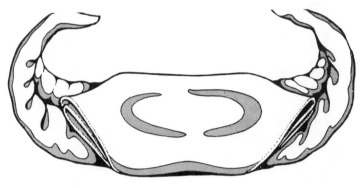

1. Place a square of aluminum foil in the center of a napkin.

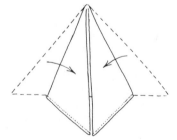

2. Fold in half.

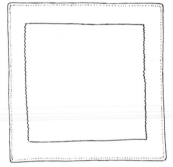

3. Fold top left and right corners to bottom center.

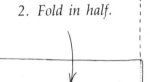

4. Fold again in the same manner.

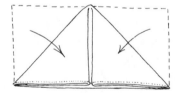

5. And again.

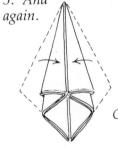

Continued on next page

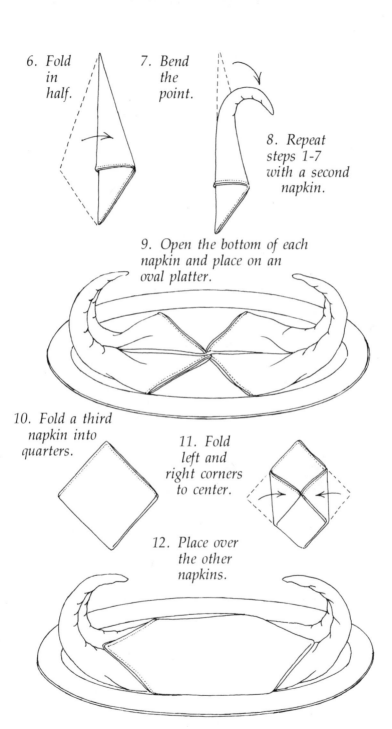

6. Fold in half.

7. Bend the point.

8. Repeat steps 1-7 with a second napkin.

9. Open the bottom of each napkin and place on an oval platter.

10. Fold a third napkin into quarters.

11. Fold left and right corners to center.

12. Place over the other napkins.

Four Petal Flower

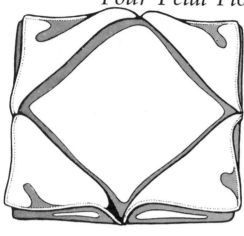

1. Fold corners to center.

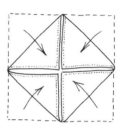

2. Hold in place at the center, and turn the napkin over.

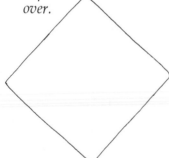

3. Fold corners to center.

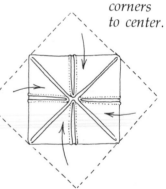

4. Hold in place at the center, and turn the napkin over again.

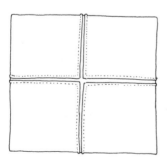

5. Fold center points to outside corners.

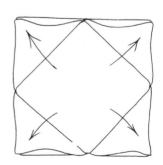

Eight Petal Flower

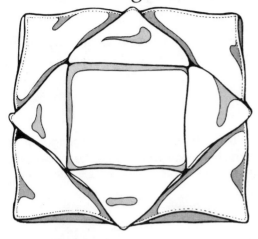

Repeat steps
1-4 of the
four petal
flower.

5. Fold corners
   to center.

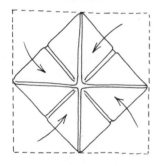

6. Hold in place at
   the center, and
   turn the
   napkin
   over.

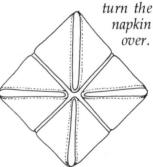

7. Fold center points
   to outside corners.

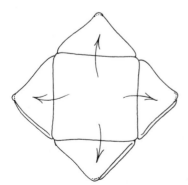

8. Place in
   the center
   of a four
   petal
   flower.

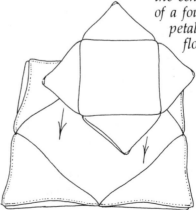

PARTY IDEAS

Menus and place cards can be hand lettered by an art student at a minimal cost and enhance a formal table as well as reducing confusion.

Some music, a guitar or harp, played by a teenager in an adjoining room creates a charming surprise. Ask the musician to arrive in the middle of the meal to produce the maximum effect.

When making a flower arrangement the flowers should not extend beyond $1/5$ of the width of the table.

The more formal the dinner, the greater will be the absence of color. The color comes from the china and the food and wine, not from the table linens.

Do not select highly perfumed flowers for the dining table. They will overpower the aroma of the food and the fragrance of the wine.

A candle in the middle of an artichoke, red cabbage or bunch of asparagus, makes an inexpensive but dramatic center-piece.

Make a centerpiece by piling beautiful oranges into a pyramid. Hold the oranges in place with bamboo skewers or florist picks. Use the oranges on a floral cloth.